Quick
and
Slow
Animals

by Barbara J. Behm
Illustrated by Martin Camm

Gareth Stevens Publishing
MILWAUKEE

For a free color catalog describing Gareth Stevens Publishing's list of high-quality books and multimedia programs, call 1-800-542-2595 (USA) or 1-800-461-9120 (Canada). Gareth Stevens Publishing's Fax: (414) 225-0377.

Library of Congress Cataloging-in-Publication Data

Behm, Barbara J., 1952-
 Quick and slow animals / by Barbara J. Behm; illustrated by Martin Camm.
  p. cm. — (Animal opposites)
 Includes index.
 Summary: Introduces ten animals that can be distinguished by how fast they move, including the sea lion, sloth, kiwi, slow loris, gibbon, manatee, springhare, snail, cheetah, and tortoise.
 ISBN 0-8368-2461-X (lib. bdg.)
 1. Animals—Miscellanea—Juvenile literature. [1. Animals.] I. Camm, Martin, ill. II. Title. III. Series: Animal opposites (Milwaukee, Wis.)
 QL49.B5363 1999
 590—dc21   99-31623

This North American edition first published in 1999 by
Gareth Stevens Publishing
1555 North RiverCenter Drive, Suite 201
Milwaukee, WI 53212 USA

This edition © 1999 by Gareth Stevens, Inc. Created with original © 1997 by Horus Editions Limited, a division of Award Publications Limited, 1st Floor, 27 Longford Street, London NW1 3DZ, U.K. Additional end matter © 1999 by Gareth Stevens, Inc.

Cover illustrations: a sea lion and a sloth

Printed in the United States of America

1 2 3 4 5 6 7 8 9 03 02 01 00 99

Contents

Sea Lion

The sea lion is a quick animal.

The sea lion swims faster than most other animals. It is very graceful in the water.

Sea lions
feed on fish,
octopus,
and squid.

Sloth

*The sloth is a
slow animal.*

The sloth sleeps about
fifteen hours every day.
It hangs upside-down in
the treetops.

Kiwi

The kiwi is a quick animal.

The kiwi is a bird that lives in New Zealand. It cannot fly, but it runs very fast.

Kiwis
hunt for
food
at night.

Slow Loris

The slow loris is a slow animal.

The slow loris is never in a hurry. It lives in the jungles and bamboo forests of Asia.

Slow lorises hide
in trees.

Gibbon

*The gibbon is a
quick animal.*

The gibbon is the
acrobat of the animal
world. It swings from
branch to branch.

Gibbons
balance
with their
arms.

13

Manatee

The manatee is a slow animal.

The manatee lives in rivers and along the seashore. It feeds on water plants.

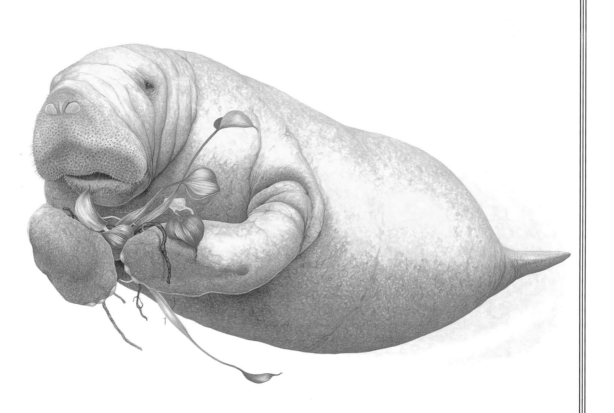

Manatees can stay under
water a long time.

Springhare

*The springhare
is a quick animal.*

The springhare is often
hunted by other animals.
It must get away fast!

Springhares hop
on their back legs.

Cheetah

The cheetah is a quick animal.

The cheetah is the fastest runner in the world. It lives on the plains in Africa.

Cheetahs run short
distances at top speed.

Tortoise

The tortoise is a slow animal.

The tortoise walks very slowly. It has to carry a heavy shell on its back everywhere it goes.

Giant tortoises can live
two hundred years.

Glossary

balance: to steady oneself by putting weight evenly onto both sides.

graceful: moving in a smooth, flowing manner.

jungles: forested areas in warm, tropical regions.

plains: a large, rolling area of level ground that does not have trees.

squid: a ten-armed mollusk, related to the octopus, that lives in the sea.

Index